Songs for Each Mood

vol II

Follow the Author:

Twitter: MichaelTavon
Instagram: @michaeltavonpoetry
Tikitok: MichaeltavonPoetry

Michael Tavon

Amazon Self-Publishing

Kindle Direct Publishing

Songs for Each Mood II

Other Works

Poetry Collections

Nirvana: Pieces of Self-Healing vol 1
Nirvana: Pieces of Self-Healing vol.2
A Day Without Sun
Songs for Each Mood
Don't Wait Til I Die to Love Me
Dreaming in a Perfect World
The Pisces

Fiction Novels

God is a Woman
Far from Heaven

Affirmations and Quotes
Heal, Inspire, Love w/ Moonsouldchild
Self-Talks w/ Moonsoulchild

Michael Tavon

Dear Reader:

Before you begin reading, there's a playlist waiting for you on my YouTube channel (Michael Tavon). If you are unable to find it, feel free to send me a message. I promise I will get back to you asap!

Songs for Each Mood II

Michael Tavon

Press Play

Playlist I: Random Feels

Change The World | Michael Jackson

My friend, Let's heal and grow
Together we can,
Change the world
Do you know
The power your voice holds?

Police stop pouring bullets
Like raindrops,
The violence must stop.
We shouldn't have
to become an army
To survive against cops.

Erase our memory
History is a lie
Teach the truth,
Reprogram our minds

Free the children,
Trapped in cages
They aren't killers or rapists
Why tame them?

Together, We can change
the systems ways
Hopefully, one day,
This world will be a better place

Begin | Shallou

After years of being buried six feet deep in grief, it's time to climb out of that hole and fall in love with the person you've bloomed into after the storm. Life will never be the same; accept the change. The tears you once shed helped you transform into what you see in the mirror today. Now, you are far greater than you were before. Grief didn't break you; it shaped you.

Take Me Home | Poolside

Anything you desire
Your mind has
the power to manifest,
so instead of yearning
for objects that feed the ego
and starve the soul
envision a heart that beats softer
like a feather drifting in the wind
after grief releases its grip on you,
Close your eyes and envision,
your dreams becoming a reality
after self-doubt
stops living in your mind rent-free,
once you finally recognize your worth
better yet, imagine a life
where inner peace
has become second nature,
because you've learned how to manage
your reaction to any force that tries
to knock you off your balance.
you have the power
to create the life you deserve

Bee | Burbank

Your heart must shatter into pieces
Before discovering peace, again

The thunderstorms
in your mind must settle,
Before feeling the calm winds

The process of healing
is allowing your dark clouds to rain
Without hurrying
Your sunshine

No matter how long it takes
You must feel to heal

Mother nature doesn't
rush her process
Neither should you

Everything that happens,
Serves as a purpose
For your growth

Open | Rhye

Vivid dreams of you

Next to the soft sound of rain

All the bliss I need

E.W.T.R.T.W | Tears for Fears

I don't know who needs to hear this, but you are beautiful the way you were designed. Crafted by the hands of time, there's no need to obsess over what you perceive as flaws when you stare into the mirror. Your body doesn't have to be paper-thin. Your skin is allowed to have blemishes like the sky. Stop pressuring yourself to resemble the facades you see on social media and tv. Beauty resides in many shapes and hues.

Change ur Mind | Sarcastic Sounds

Life is the movie
I didn't audition for
But was cast in
Without a script
now I'm forced to adlib

When the cameras roll
My eyes squint in the bright lights
My breath leaves my lungs
As my heart tries to escape my chest
I'm clueless
So I pretend to know what I'm doing
To keep from looking stupid

The most thrilling part to this,
There are no mulligans
Or edits in posts
My bloopers and failed
Stunts will get left on the reel
For the world to witness
The audience gets to see
The embarrassment on my face
And the bruises
from performing my own stunts
I may screw up a thousand times
But I'm going to
Play this role with my truth
that's what I was born to do

Pov | Ariana Grande

You say it's rare
For a man to want to see you
When your face is bare
unkempt hair
And no mascara when you stare
Well I don't care

I want to see the beauty of you
when you wake up
without fake lashes and makeup
So Let's layup
Be lazy

With your hair all tangled
and wavy in your grey sweats
from old navy Baby,
to you, it sounds crazy or foreign
You think the natural you is boring
I think it's worth exploring

The deep wonders of your body
I must explore,
Take a tour

Through your past scars
Trace over your stretch marks
Strum through your hair
like a Spanish guitar

open up, be vulnerable with me
let's sync energies
so we can glow the way
we're meant to be

I mean every syllable
When I say I love you
I'll write your name in the sky
So only God is above you

Day n Nite | Kid Cudi

Don't waste another second being grounded by fear; set your passion free. Allow those pretty wings to feel the air beneath them. Fly wild in the sky until your dreams are within your reach.

Pacing | Tep No

When your mind begins to feel like a playground for
negative thoughts to crowd and socialize, find a space
where you can settle down before anxiety pays a visit.
Put your phone down, sit still like a frog on a lily pad,
and inhale. Find an open field and bellow from the
bottom of your gut to the sky. Leave those negative
thoughts behind by chasing the sunset ahead. Do
what you must to clear your mind.

Another Day in Paradise | Phil Collins

I apologize,
For being a deadbeat friend

My image was a mirage,
For your eyes to believe
The façade I created,
My life was all smoke and mirrors
In pictures
I wore my smile like
the latest fashion
With inspirational
quotes as my captions
Denzel would be proud
Because I became an Oscar-worthy actor,
They say the best medicine
is laughter so I became
the world's biggest clown
I didn't want to break character,
 I ignored your calls
And happy birthday wishes

See, I got so good
at playing hide n seek
with depression
I lost sight of who I was
And I didn't want you
To help find me

I didn't want
My emotions
To be a burden,
So I went ghost,
I know, being there
Is what friends are for
But I wanted you to fly
Without me,

Now that I'm back
I know,
Things will never be the same
I hope you understand
Depression is a lonely game,
And I defeated it in silence

I take all the blame
If you allow,
I'll introduce the new me
Into your life

Over the Moon | The Marias

I will discover the place
Where my heart is loved
I will find the space
Where my energy is fed with light
And I will make my new home there

You Broke my Heart | Current Joys

Where I'm from the sun doesn't
give a damn
About personal space when
she's on a tirade
She will curse you
to your face
And tells you to go back inside.
You'd burn
if you don't listen
The sidewalks feel
like burning coal
On your bare soles
And the leaves never switch
Colors like a crip or blood
They just remain
Green, all 4 seasons,
It's shaped like a gun
You'd understand why
If you live there,
A wild jungle
Where alligators roam territories
like gangbangers
this place,
We may have grown apart
But this will always be home,

Inside My Head | Toro Y Moi

You won't bloom
into the best version
 of yourself
if you keep trying
grow where the sun doesn't shine

Without U | Beach Goons

I lied to myself so many times
I was living a double life
To shrug off my anguish
Deceit became a second language
Suddenly, my world became
more fiction than reality
Escapism was my favorite
Defense mechanism
And falling in love with my crushes
from the first hello
To see how fast they'd
Break my heart
Became my favorite sport
I did all of this to avoid
The man in the mirror
I was afraid to confront
My demons
I knew I had to change
and it was the furthest thing
From easy

Last Day | Shallou

If dementia
finds a home inside
My mind,
Please, let me die
I refuse
To live a life
Where I can't, find
The words to write

Michael Tavon

Lost in Yesterday | Tame Impala

Your tea has gone cold
Daydreaming over yesterdays
Long gone

You play the same old songs
Hoping the memories
Come back home

You try to move on
with your foot stuck in the mud

you try to remain strong
while slowly breaking down

you're convinced
your best days are behind
living with scenes of yesterday
playing on rewind

You'll never learn to let go
When the past is strangled by your palms
Set the past free
Today is where you belong

<u>Stay Safe</u> | <u>Rhye</u>

Hello, my friend
How's your heart and mind?
Does the light inside
You still shine?
If not, you may
have some of mine,

I know you wish to hibernate
The day away
when the sun awakes and says *hey*

I know yesterday was a gamble
And you lost every bet you played,

I'm here to say,
It's okay,
You'll be okay,
Each day is a game,
You won't win them all

So how's your heart?
How's your mind

I'm not asking to hear you,
I'm here to FEEL you

Everything I Wanted | Billie Eilish

(After Lucille Clifton)

What the mirror said:
You, a whole universe
There is beauty behind your darkness
Guidance in your light,
People marvel when they gaze at you
The way they do, stars & the moon
Why do you refuse to see the same?
Dear human,
Perfection is a myth
Those insecurities will swallow you
Like a dark hole
If you don't learn
To love the galaxies inside you

Thank You | Dito

Family isn't measured in blood
It's a life bond
One must earn.

Just because we are
Two fruits from one tree
Doesn't mean
we have the same core

Will you be there
When I need you most?

Sometimes,
relatives are more estranged
Than strangers

why should I trust you,
Because you have the same name as I do?

Tadow | Masago & FKJ

Heartbreak painted you
With its darkest hues
But gander at beautiful art
It made of you

Grief carved you
From the hardest clay
Now, look at the
Sculpture, made
from the pain in you

you think
these are the
last of your days
but your best days are still ahead

so, cry but stay strong
Let those tears flow
Pain doesn't break you
It shapes you

That's the Way it is | Phil Collins

Hometown woes,

The place you
know oh so well
Is your home by default
It's your home
Because you were planted there,
you didn't choose
To bloom in this toxic soil
But you made the best of it

Your hometown soil,
It is often the worst
Ground for growth,
Yet you still branched out

Some friends and family
Will let you fester in the sun
Without watering your roots
Then question why,
You can't provide
air or shade for them

Some locals believe,
They have your life figured out
Through,
Rumors whispered in the wind
they tear your leaves,
And swing from your branches
Until you begin to break

And wonder why
You aren't sturdy
enough to carry their weight

Just because
you were born there
That doesn't mean you
have to let them drain you

Find peace in a new home
You were born with the
Courage to do so

Fear | Drake

Be softer on your heart
Life is hard enough,
Self-doubt is a prison
Release yourself from its cuffs

You deserve so much more
Than what you settle for
But you refuse
To evacuate the comfort zone

You're drowning in sorrow
Suffocated by despair
Breathe in, exhale
Be aware, be there

Stop beating yourself up,
The past you can't change
Heal from your mistakes
Get ready for a new day

Echo | Incubus

A sinner in dimensions
Sill perfectly me
Never regret my mistakes
Wear them on my sleeve
Set my burdens free
I can finally breath

Take Me Home | Phil Collins

When that loud cracking sound
Echoed the neighborhood
Fear and adrenaline
coursed through our veins
As we morphed
into ghetto track stars
Running for safety
In full stride
never looked behind
We just hoped
We Made it to
the finish line alive,
We understood
Why our parents
Wanted us home
Before the streetlights
Came on

P.Y.T (Original) | Michael Jackson

Sometimes I
I wake up
in the middle of the night,
to see if her belly still rises,
she sleeps so wild
Her body contorted
Like a serpent

She awakes with
Confusion in her eyes,
Wondering why
My finger is under her nose
"The hell are you doing?" She asks.
"Making sure you're still alive,"
I roll over and shut my eyes.
with the peace of knowing
She's still breathing next to me.

Jethro | Thundercat

The harshest reality to come to terms with is realizing you're outgrowing your environment, friends, and loved ones. We hold these bonds so close because, in a way, they made us who we are, but there will come a time when you'll notice that things are no longer the same. The life you once knew will slowly drift away as you grow, and part of you will try so hard to hold on, but you can't save everything from your past. As heartbreaking as this may sound, everyone you know will not fit in with the path you chose. Accept this fact and never look back.

TailWhip | Men I Trust

I no longer feel empty
When given space
Solitude is my best friend,
Because loneliness became bliss
the moment I fell in love with myself

It is True | Tame Impala

Yesterday doesn't want you anymore
but tomorrow will greet you
when the sunrises
Today is here, now
So please, my friend
Appreciate this day
before you let
Time slip away
By chasing after yesterdays
That left you behind
And running away from
the tomorrows
that are eager to meet you

Peaches | Justin Bieber

Love-drunk, between messy sheets
too lazy to dress the bed fancy
from the night before

she tickles my side and giggles
when I shiver like a spider
crawled down my shirt

deeply in love,
how we still flirt,

the way
Her fingertips know
where to go,
It's evident they
Took time to learn
My soft spots

The neighbors know her name
by the way I yell, "stop, babe."
loud enough to make
the walls shake

Even when
I pretend to despise her ass
I always appreciate
Every moment she makes me laugh

The Difference | Flume & Toro Y Moi

The inside jokes,
and body telepathy
We speak a language,
Outsiders can't understand
in this nation of two ~
we love by our own rules
rewritten the definition of religion
we don't live by a strict system
no raincheck dreams
in this land we live
Our true bliss comes
When we see each other win
Our love,
Never been battle-tested,
Our foundation was set
In faith and trust,
We don't give a damn
What the world thinks of us

Playlist II: R&B: Past & Present

I Care 4 U | Aaliyah

I know today was a thief that tried to
steal your peace,
But you're still here.
You run on low energy
like the battery on your phone
and the bags of stress under your eyes
are getting heavier
by the second, so
I won't ask how was work
because the answer won't be,
"the greatest day of my life,"
Nor will I ask how was school,
because the answer won't be,

"I've learned so many valuable things."
Instead, I will ask
How's your heart?
Does it beat stronger, or is it tearing apart?
Did you find fresh air to inhale
When responsibilities tried to suffocate
You with its bare hands?

My next question, "how's your mind."
Tell me the thoughts that simmer,
Like heatwaves.
Are you on the verge of breaking down
Or did u find your crown?
Tell me the inside jokes
You keep to yourself?

Michael Tavon

Your heart and mind
Is what I deeply care for
So tell me, my friend
How's your heart?
How's your mind

Care | Sonder

The true cure for homesickness
Is realizing
The life you once thought
You couldn't live without
Is the life
That was slowly killing you

So don't feel guilty
For finding a new home

Sometimes,
You gotta
Leave it all behind
To find,
Who you truly are

Snowchild | The Weeknd

I often wonder what stories
will my loved ones tell
When my body lies stiff
Like a tree torn from the root

What memories will they
bring to light
Before my flesh and bones decompose
and become earth food

Will they recall a moment
When we laughed until
our diaphragms knotted
Like tangled shoe strings

Will they mention
The first time we met?
And how awkward
they thought I was
until they REALLY
Got to know me

Who will strum everyone's
Heartstrings like a violin
By telling a heartfelt
Story of how
I changed their life?

And which stranger
will be there

To remind everyone
How important it is
to Smile and be kind
Because our brief interaction
Brightened their day
When their clouds were grey

I know it's strange
To think about
what people will say
at my funeral

But my curious mind
Wants to know
how people genuinely feel
About me

Because I will never know
How some people truly
feel about me until I no longer
Have the breath to say thank you.

Doesn't Really Matter | Janet Jackson

"I aspire to be like you."
I said to the moon.
"Amid the darkness
You possess the power
To rise high and provide
The light this cynical world
needs every night."

She laughed and said,
"you have that same power too,
it's in your smile."

<u>The Moon & The Sky | Sade</u>

There are some good people
I wish I was a better friend to
But my depression and anxiety
Said I was unworthy of
Keeping good people around,
So I drifted away
Like a feather in the wind
I was convinced
They would be better
without my dark clouds
raining over their flowers,
And they didn't
Deserve to feel the thunderstorms
Rumbling inside me,
So every invite
To hang out was declined
And when I changed
my number
They didn't receive
a text from me
I knew, my presence
would only hold them down
Even though I needed
them around
Sometimes, I wish I had told them
What was real
Instead, I was ashamed,
And pushed them away
I was taught

Michael Tavon

"depression is a weakness,"
And "boys don't cry."
And I thought I was strong
By not letting them
see me breakdown
One day,
I hope they read this poem
And understand
I'd love to be friends again

Trust | Brent Faiyaz

The way I create more problems
Than I resolve
 I'd be an awful mechanic

Instead of fixing the issues
I have today I fixate
On the problems
That don't exist at all

My mind is far from
a well-oiled machine,
I manufacture more breakdowns,
Than the average unethical mechanic,
But not on purpose

part of me
fears what the future holds
So I sabotage my joy by overthinking,
Until I miss out on the moments
I should appreciate

I should trust myself more
I need to stop making
life harder than
It already is

Burn | Usher

She was twice my age,
My dad's ex-girlfriend
With cheap cigar lips
and beer breath
Her kiss...Oh her kiss
tasted liked cat piss
When she shoved her tongue
down my throat
Vomit began to rise
Like moss on trees
I wanted to leave
But boys don't turn pussy down, right?
I took a swig from her
E&J bottle swallowed my pride,
And allowed her to have her way
When I told her to stop, she went faster,
Shame took over my body,
I could no longer perform,
She asked *what's wrong*
I said, *I can't do this no more*
Two days later, I felt the wrath
Of my mistake
A mistake I didn't want to make,
On the bathroom floor
I ached with pain
There was no fire
but I still felt the flame,

Rose in the Dark | Cleo Sol

The barber,
Who knows how to carve beauty
From any surface,
With clippers and a blade
Is an artist

The janitor,
Who performs magic
Tricks with a mop
To make stains disappear
Is an artist, too

The drive-thru lady with the animated
voice is an artist as well

The mailperson delivering in the rain
The cashier,
Whose been on her feet for 8 hours
The restaurant chef,
Tweaking off the fourth can of monster
The landscapist with sunburn
Are all artists,

Never disrespect the people
Who dedicates their time
Making your life easier
Especially when they bring joy
To your life

John Redcorn | Sir

Some people often find themselves
Down the rabbit hole
of negativity
when scrolling their timelines
fueling the impulse
to respond to trolls
gangbanging on keyboards
with strangers
ten thousand miles away,
wasting time being twitter patrols,
policing every opinion
that triggers them
Instagram bandits,
Talking reckless,
In the comment section
Of celebrities
To everyone who disagrees with them
then call social media toxic
while ignoring the artists
trying to make
a name for themselves
or scroll past sound healers,
and health teachers.
Social media ain't toxic
It's the people you follow,
The content you consume,
the posts you react to

Missing you | Case

To find the person who loves every layer of your being after unraveling your fears and doubts is the rarest connection life has to offer. So, when you find that type of love, don't let it slip away. You won't find it twice in one lifetime.

<u>Missing You | Case</u>

Without you,

I wouldn't go far
Like wheels without a car
I wouldn't shine as bright,
Like the night sky without stars

I'd be a compass without direction
Lost without your affection
Like a call with bad connection,
I wouldn't hear your joy and blessings

My love is too strong
To ever let you go
No bad soil,
We will always grow

A dead man could feel
Your love is rare
Push you away,
I wouldn't dare

They say love is a gamble
Which is kinda true
I won't take any bet
That would risk losing you

<u>Wishing on a Star | Rose Royce</u>

Sometimes we create the illusion of joy
With smiles and laughter,
hoping we're clever enough
To make the world believe the stunt

We try to make sadness disappear
By hiding it being a wall
And tapping it three times

Sometimes depression
turns us into magicians,
Because reality is too painful
To deal with

All for You | Janet Jackson

Do you believe in forever, baby?
It wouldn't be a waste of time
if we tried
even if we fall short
our love would still last a lifetime

<u>Full Moon | Brandy</u>

Poetry doesn't have to hide behind pretentious rhymes and long-winded lines anymore. It can be raw; it can be subtle. It can be loud; it can be humble. Poetry graduated from a language to a nuanced emotion. Poetry is a baby's laughter or hearing the first 'I love you' roll off your crush's tongue. It's the snow begging you to make angels with her. It's the bliss you find when you feel alone. It's the therapy you find while grieving. It's licking a popsicle as it melts under the sun; it's watching sunflowers bloom. It's the words that make your heart cry when watching This is Us. Poetry doesn't have to be perfect to be good because poetry is what we feel.

Video | India Arie

The moon has different moods, too
Some nights
she hides behind the clouds
And some nights she
Shines at the forefront
Sometimes she shares the stage
With the stars
And sometimes she performs
As a solo act

No matter what phase the moon
Is in she finds a way
To show the world
Her beautiful imperfections
We, as humans marvel
at the moon's
phases and hues
Round, red, crescent, blue,
And I ask why can't
We love ourselves
And each other the way
we love the moon?

Yesterday Princess | Stanley Clark

You build facades
Around your heart
To protect you from harm
But in the long run
You're becoming
numb to the truth

You gotta feel to heal
be real with yourself
Stop living in denial

If your pride
Is the wall
Keeping you from crying
Let that guard down
And let those tears flow

Sometimes, crying
Is the medicine needed
To cure a broken heart

<u>Moonchild | The Other Side</u>

The sun loves me,
I can tell,
By the way
It keeps me warm
But never burns

The clouds love me,
They keep me outta harm's way
When thunder
Commands me to stay home
I know rain will pour
So it's best for me
to stay off the road

The moon loves me,
I know this,
By the way
it's been my nightlight
Since the days
I was afraid of the dark outside
And the darkness that
Lived inside me

Same Old Song | The Weeknd

A narcissist's greatest trick is luring in empaths like the pied piper with empty promises of providing the love they desire. The masters of disguise, hiding behind wicked smiles, breaking down walls to get what they want. Empaths struggle with noticing the red flags because they view their relationships through rose-colored frames. Playing by the narcissist's game, empaths put on their capes to save their lover from themselves. In the end, the empath drains their love until there's nothing in their heart to give, while the narcissist moves on to find another victim to lure in with the same old songs.

Leave it all Behind | Foreign Exchange

The same way a tree feels
its dead leaves departing
From its limbs.
I feel old friends
Slipping out of my grip
just like the tree
I won't mope
Or lose hope
Over dead pieces
And old feelings
Instead,
I will smile at the sun
Knowing now I have more room
For stronger roots to grow

<u>Everything | Mary J Blige</u>

The moment we met
For you, I opened my heart
Love became our home

Stay Flo | Solange
(When I was a teen)

Boys bottled their emotions
tossed them into the ocean,
with the feeling of
Seafoam hopelessness
While the world watched
them drown in the open

When they cried for a lifeguard
No one helped them to shore

Boys don't cry
Tears are too feminine
Forced to be tough
When softness was the best remedy

when boys can't cry
they become class clowns
to mask the pain

When boys are told
It's soft to be sad
They turn other kids
Into punching bags

When boys are told
'It's gay' to share feelings
They numb themselves with drugs
And confuse it with healing

Dreaming of You | Selena

There we were,
Two dreamers lying
Side by side
In the middle of the night
With our eyes shut
Like car doors
My snow white
Rested still, on her back,
I turned to my side,
& placed her cheek in my palm
my lips found hers
Like they were searching for days
I kissed her with electricity
Flowing through my lips
Her eyes opened,
In shock, she pushed me off
And yelled,
"What the fuck are you doing?"
 I snapped back into reality
And said, "I don't know."
She left the bed to take a piss.
I drifted back into a dream,
It wasn't until the morning
I realized the silly fairy tale stunt
I tried to pull when she asked
"Did you kiss me when I was asleep?"

If You Think You're Lonely | Bobby Womack

You are unpredictable like the ocean
But I never fear drowning
in your wave of emotions
When you open up
I hold my breath,
dive in, allowing my skin
to get drenched in your energy,
After my body soaks,
I yearn for more

I'm not the best swimmer
But your currents always
carry me to shore
most people fear getting
consumed by your massive waves
Not I, I admire your intensity
I'm allured by your mystery

And I will always choose to swim
Knowing you would never
let me drown

I'll Be Around | The Spinners

I was so addicted to
The feeling of being wanted
I latched onto
every friendly smile
And fell in love with every hello
When the inevitable goodbyes
Arrived I was left
Feeling lower than dirt
This drug, I loved
Because loneliness was the ghost
I was afraid to sleep next to
So I shared my bed with
other lonely souls
Hoping a one-night stand
Would turn into
A happily ever after
This drug slowly drained my heart
And left many scars
it was slowly killing me
And I knew it

River | Leon Bridges

(Aka: Thug Story)

Trying to find work
Has become a full time
A job I loath
My cell phone remains silent and alone
No callbacks received
Is it 'cause my name
is blacker than lava stones?
Is it because my home
Is located near liquor stores?
Every hour I open
Email responses
That begins with
"We regret to inform you,"
And end with
"Decided to go
with a more experienced candidate."

Experience?
How much fucking experience does
One need to bag groceries
Or flip burgers
My baby needs formula,
lights are dim
I shiver in the shower,
Warm water gone.

So I push weight,
Like bodybuilders
To stack dollar figures

I sell what makes
people rot and die
To keep my family alive

Until I'm in cuffs,
trapped in a cage do my time,
Released back into the wild,
A job becomes harder to find
With felon attached to my name
I repeat the cycle
Trapped in the system's game

I'm a thug, they say,
I'm a thug, they claim
Maybe I am a thug
A thug, they made

.

Bye Bipolar | Brandy

My cousins played
"The floor is lava."
So often because their mother
Was a volcano,
When her lava hot temper
went flaring
They learned how to
Run for cover
Before she burned them

They played
hide and seek so often
it was the only time
Their mother would participate
When she locked herself
In her cold dark room
And couldn't be found for days

They played these games,
Not for fun but survival
These boys became products
of a broken childhood

Then they grew into men
With childish minds
One played cops and robbers
For a living,

Songs for Each Mood II

Now behind bars

The other,
Played 'doctor'
with his little sister,
Some say he was schizophrenic
Before he went missing

My cousins played
These childhood games
Until society labeled them
Thugs and sickos,
In some cases, Rightfully so

what they don't know
My cousins played
these childhood games
To protect each other
Because their mother is bi-polar
And home was never fun

Above and Beyond | Jhene Aiko

You may have fallen
into the dark hole of heartbreak,
but don't let the grief bury you alive.
You are strong enough
to climb to the top without them

Borrowed Time | Malia

You have
a million reasons to cry,
let those tears flow,
Amid your rain,
I hope you know
There's always a reason to smile

If You Let Me | Sinead Harnett

I hope,
40 years from now
we're looking at old pictures
Of our young love
Smiling at how things
Never changed.

Weight in Gold | Gallant

Planted in the soil of hope and mistakes
You've grown through many seasons
From the seed you used to be
You are not the rose you once were
You are not
The flower everyone wants you to be
If they love you the way
They claim they do
they wouldn't pluck your petals
When they see you bloom

So I Lie | Miguel

I denied my depression
Like a bad check
Paying the price,
For my mistakes left me
in a million-minute debt
I shied away from mirrors
Blind to my scars
In fear of seeing the naked truth
Couldn't see my flaws
Footloose, dancin' with my demons
I got drunk to hide my feelings

Shuffled my deck,
Gambling with the cards
Life dealt me I lost to the real me

I thought ignoring depression
Would make it go away
Instead, it remained
Until I changed my ways

Summer Rain | Carl Thomas

Aren't we all tired of love poems?

Who needs another
puzzle of words pieced together
To create the perfect image
That fits the description of a four-letter word

This love poem
doesn't make sense,
Neither does love
But it feels so damn good

Love is like water
We can't survive without it,

Aren't we all tired of love poems?
Like this one,
Metaphors and rhymes
About heartbeats
skipping like metronome
Felling lost, finding your home

Even if we are tired of love poems,
We still read them
Love poems give hope
They help us believe
Somewhere in this sad, lonely hell,
There's love to be found

Michael Tavon

Rain | SWV

Every day with you
Is beautiful Deja vu
Ecstasy still rises
with the sun
Every morning,
we wake up
our eyes never grow tired
of greeting

I could rewind
the times we share
in my mind and smile
like it was the first time

Your love feels familiar,
and foreign like a place
I've been before
But always discover
New ways to explore

You remind me,
Of a pleasant dream
I feel but can't touch
when I wake up
to my pleasant déjà vu

For Us | DVSN

On one bended knee
I bow to my lunar queen

The irony, of me
The man of a million
metaphors and verses
Too nervous
to summon the courage
To say four simple words

The thunder in my stomach
Begins to settle once my eyes
Bear witness to the
Cherry blush covering
the constellations on your face

Your smile,
Reminds me of the night sky
When it shines

time freezes
when *yes* rolls off your tongue
Who knew a three-letter word
could last a lifetime

Tremors from my hand
As I try to slide the
rose gold ring
To the bottoms of your finger
But it gets stuck

Michael Tavon

At the second knuckle
We chuckle
Just like the ring
Lodged on your finger
Our love is a bond,
Attached, together forever.

Doesn't Really Matter | Janet Jackson

I fell in love with
The Lisa Bonets & Sades
While ignoring
Regina Halls and Nia Longs

"You got a type," My friends said.
"Not by choice," I respond.
 The Lynns from Girlfriends

Seemed to want me more
Than the Gabrielle Union's next door

"You love those, curly-headed light skins,"

they said.

Well, the Kelly Rolands
Said I was too weird,
or soft or not hood enough

while the Beyonces
Fell in love
With my quirks and charm

I was labeled as the guy
Who had a 'preference.'
When that was the only
preference that preferred me.

Michael Tavon

Ready | Frank Ocean

If your walls could talk
What would they say about me?
I hope something sweet

Sittin' up in my Room | Brandy

We've been conditioned to believe
Love is a constant battle
To see who will make it out
The crossfire alive

Nights of tear-soaked pillowcases,
open ended conversations,
words used as swords
to rip each other openly
Hoping, love is strong enough
To prevail

What if I told you
Real love ain't a war?
It doesn't have
To break you down
to make your relationship stronger

Real love is soft,
The type of softness
That gently unravels,
The doubt and fear
Entangled in your mind

The wars you endure
Will prepare you for the love
you've been waiting for
You'll notice the difference
once you find it

Michael Tavon

Mercy Mercy Me | Marvin Gaye

I used to watch
a thousand ways to die
Laughing at how
Some people treat life
As if they were granted mulligans
sometimes funny,
I thought
What if they made
A thousand ways to die
for black people
I presume
Ratings would be low
Episodes would be cut short
Since being black
Is a game of craps
We don't have to gamble
With our lives to die

I Get So Lonely | Janet Jackson

Sometimes being black is a lonely place,
With stereotypes and microaggressions
Painted on the walls

living here gets exhausting,
outsiders only visit
when tragedy happens

Slogans like *solidarity* &
Black Lives Matter
written on the ceilings
they even chant with us too,
until tomorrow arrives
they leave us with the mess
of yesterday to clean up

they love our food, they love the words
that flow from our tongues in rhythms
they love our clothes and the way our
skin looks in them

they whitewash our culture in bleach
maybe the way we live, is too dirty for them.

oh, how they love,
this place called blackness
but they hate the people
that live inside

Being black is a lonely place
Where we learned how to thrive.

Michael Tavon

All This Love | Donell Jones

Peel off your layers
Expose the truth
Beyond your skin
Let me dive inside
The oceans of you
Show me the space
Others were afraid to explore
Speak your love language
I'm all ears, I won't ignore

If | Janet Jackson

I would've missed
The answer to my prayers,
If I had left your message
On read

Sometimes,
That special someone
Is in your inbox
waiting for you
to give them a chance

Michael Tavon

Miss You So | Frank Ocean

I'm thankful
I never have to miss you,
No daydreaming,
Of your gentle kisses
Because you're always next to me

I don't have to
waste hours staring
Into your pictures
Reminiscing the
times we shared,
Because our love
still rise like spring flowers,

Loneliness stopped
sleeping next to me
The night you shared
A bed with me.
Insomnia said goodbye
When you entered my life

There's no dust
To be blown off our book.
Because chapters of our story
Are still being written

I never have to forget you,
Heartache doesn't exist between us.
Our memories are too sweet
And your presence
Is my greatest gift

Why Don't We Fall in Love | Amerie

Nights feel darker
When I sleep alone,
I get lost in thought
Because I have nowhere to go
Without you, emptiness is the dark hole,
I refuse to fall asleep next to,
Again, if I did,
would you grab
my hand and save me?

Sleeping next to you
Provides peace of mind
Now, when darkness falls
you hold me down like gravity
Using your love as a force
Protecting my sanity

I know, my loneliness
is not your problem to fix
while I resolve this feeling

please be patient, keep me company?
Sometimes, affection is the best medicine
when I show symptoms
of heartache

♪

Kiss me More | Doja Cat

My only desire
Is to ensure
Your heart never beats
Heavy with doubt
The love I provide
Is the kind
That will
Keep you satisfied

𝄢

So Much More | Xavier Omar

Our love,
Endless like waterfalls
Eternal like time
Soul bonds
Intertwined in the rapture
Of passion,
Timeless, classic love
Two hearts beating
to the same rhythm
Our tune
The greatest
Song of all

Michael Tavon

Whipped Cream | Ari Lennox

To the parts of you
too complex to understand
I promise to forever remain
A student of your heart
I'll study your love overnight
To retain the intricacies
of your existence
I refuse to fail you,
Dropping out isn't an option
In turn,
I hope you remain patient
with me
'For I'm trying my damnedest
To excel'
in the most advanced course
of my life,
In the end it will be worth it
Because your love is perfect
Sincerely, your most dedicated pupil

Summer 2020 | Jhene Aiko

For the days when joy
seem to escape
The reach of your grasp
I will be here to lend you
some of mine
you will not feel deprived
It hurts to see you
balancing your emotions
On a tightrope of hope,
Mood swings and tears that seem
To fall, without cause
I feel helpless
'cause I can't save you
When sadness caves you in
And cuts off your air supply
We can't find the source
to your unhappiness
when S.A.D. comes around
But I vow to never give up
My shoulders are wide enough to cry on
My chest is strong enough to support
Your head when it's aching
And my arms will always
Provide warmth
When you feel cold
I have enough joy for the both of us
So please let me know
When you need some of mine

Michael Tavon

A.D.I.D.A.S | Ro James

My body inside yours
Sparks fly amid the twilight
Pleasure in the dark

You Got Me | T-Pain & Akon

Your love reminds me
Of ocean waves & raindrops
Strong & bold
Gentle & serene

Your love is like water
Without you,
There's no way
I would survive

Still Your Best | Giveon

Love, is easy on the eyes,
and I could stare into yours,
'til the moon begs me
to rest before the sun arrives

Feel | Sonder

You may feel empty
When there's a vacant space
On the other side of the bed
You try to convince yourself
loneliness will kill you
When friendships die

You latch
Onto connections
That were meant to be dropped
Like a long-distance call
But you continue
To hold on because you loath
Being left behind

Remember,
Loneliness becomes
bliss the moment
you fall in love with yourself

once you learn
how to appreciate
your own company
you will discover
the diamonds inside you
that have been buried
for so long

Michael Tavon

Ask of You | Raphael Saadiq

Your light Shines for me
On my darkest days,
& You never required
A light that shines as such
But show me where you learned
To love,
Take me there
It's only fair,
I will return
The consistency,
You've provided me

Crush | Yuna ft Usher

I never knew there
were a thousand ways
to say my name
until you fell in love with me

How the syllables flow off
your tongue like poetry

each goofy pet name
is a metaphor
layered in phrases
only you and I understand

Acura Intergurl | Frank Ocean

I'm from palm trees
Skin tanning heat
Cloud showers
Beach Waves
Sandy feet, hurricanes, & reptiles

But when I met you
I became snowstorms,
Orange leaves,
Deer, foxes, & mountains too

I'm a long way from the home
I was born
But I found a new one in you,
With you

I kiss you
With the promise
Of 100 thousand tomorrow's

Even when my ashes
Drift into the sky
I'll refuse to say goodbye

My love for you
will never die,
never die

Rain on me | Ashanti

Love is a home
That doesn't have space
For lies and heartache

Michael Tavon

Dust | Frank Ocean

I've spent years trying
to fill the imprint you left
on my mattress
with bodies that didn't matter
thoughts of you turned
to ink splatter

trying to write you
off my mind
but the words
I couldn't find,
When the ink dried
I reached for the ribbon
in the sky
that was tied for us

but it was long gone,
like a swan song
My pride couldn't admit
To being wrong
Now I'm crying alone

Step in the Name of Love | R. Kelly

Show me what that heart do
Let me dance to its tune
Because you love in a rhythm
I would love step to

Alone, on this dancefloor
I've been waiting for so long
To find someone
Who wants to dance along

I'll put your hand in mine
As our heartbeats intertwine
For a moment in forever
Slow dancing with the hands of time

Mars | Mario

Let's gently erase the space between us ~
With love floating amid the darkness
gravity draws your body close to mine
As we traverse through the universe
Between the sheets ~

Sorry | 6lack

Fall in love with who they are
Not what you expect them to be

Love them wild
Love them unconditionally
Love can't be restricted
By insecurities

Love isn't a dog,
It can't be tamed or domesticated
Love is shameless,
Love is liberating,

Find the energy that matches yours
Discover the heart that blazes
with the same coal

True love inspires
The fire that burns inside

Love is high definition,
8k resolution vivid
Love is the puzzle piece
That completes the perfect picture

Stop trying to force love
In spaces that don't fit
Your definition
Because there will always
Be something missing

When your relationship is driven
By insecurities.

If you are unable to love
Without trying to mold them,
Then it's time to let go
Your hold on them
Then figure out why
You were obsessed with controlling them

.

Playlist III: Hip Hop State of Mind

Michael Tavon

That Thing | Lauryn Hill

Girls are told to treat their virginity
Like a diamond, only give it to the boy
Who's emotionally rich enough to love them

Boys are taught to treat their virginity
Like a small stone, Toss it into the air
See where it goes

Girls are told their body is a temple
Only kings can enter
Boys are told their dick is a dart,
Aim for the bullseye
Even if you miss you'll score every time

So boys spend their youth
Trying to crack the codes
To these protected wombs

Even when she says, no
he was taught persistence is rewarded,
He travels between her legs
with guilt trips and broken promises
She thinks it's love -
But love is a sport to him

Maybe, the root of rape culture
Is the way boys are groomed
If they are taught to love their bodies
Maybe they would respect women too

NIGGER- Nas

(To all white people who think they can say it)

Nigga must be a library or hallway
The way you think there's a pass to say it.
nigga must be the latest fashion the way you dress it
with your persona

nigga must be a love song the way you sing it
from the top of your lungs
nigga must be a pretty font
The way you spell it out so lovely

Nigga must taste so sweet the way you swallow
After it rolls off your tongue
nigga must be a stand-up routine
 the way you laugh when you say it

You must think my fair brown skin
is safe space the way you say only nigga
In front of niggas that look like me,
but wouldn't fix your mouth
To spit nigga around niggas
With dark skin like the habits on nuns

You must know the word shouldn't spill
from your lips at all
But you treat it like monopoly,
Is this why you use
my best friend is black.
As your get-out-of-jail-free card?

Michael Tavon

Astronomy | BlackStar

Black life is vivid,
We live in many hues
prettier than the picture
The media painted us to be
We're not always colored in grief

Black life is:

therapy sessions in the barber's chair
Grandpa smokin' the raccoon
he popped with his BB gun
on the grill
hydrating at the water hose
After playing kill the carrier
Under the fresh sun,
drunken uncles
cursing over poker chips,
grandma's fried chicken and collard greens
showered with hot sauce,
momma braiding
sister's hair so tight
You can see what on her mind,

We were so much more than trauma
We are more layers than sorrow

We are a million little things
The outside world
would never understand
Because they belong
To us,

Where This Flower Blooms | Tyler, The Creator

The eyes of time
Blink faster than mine ~
So, I won't let precious moments
Fly by like white doves,
Released into the sky
I will unravel each gift
The universe presents to me
With pride and a smile wrapped
around my face,
Every day is a blessing,
I won't waste my sunshine
Sulking in the darkness.
I'm at peace,
This is my space
My space to be free
I'm free to be perfectly me

The People | Common

To the youth that's
Passionate about changing the world
Stop trying to 'cancel.'
the past that's
What old folks want
you to do
We need racist
Dr. Seuss
We need rapist Pepe Le Pew
Since art imitates life
art must reflect the times
nigger was sung in
Ice cream truck songs &
nursery rhymes,
"eenie meenie miny moe
catch a nigger by the toe."
comedians
Said faggot and Homo
In their jokes
And the crowd laughed
Like there was no tomorrow,
Let the younger generation
See the ugly heyday
Their grandparents lived
without rose-colored lenses
& expensive frames
History books are
Whitewashed,
filled with fiction

Let's focus on fixing
And healing
Instead of trying to erase
Everything we are afraid
to deal with
If we cancel the past
The children will
Never learn the truth,
And the bigots
Will be able to
Die not being accountable
For the horrible shit
They used to do

Michael Tavon

Stan | Eminem

One of the most complex battles
is believing in yourself
Having the strength
to realize you're good enough
After exhausting your efforts

You wear your heart
on a sleeve
Trying to show the world
why they should love you

Many scars and wounds
are inflicted
Some will be left
opened and unhealed

In the end you neglect
the only person
who matters most

If you don't believe in you
No one else will

<u>Black & Ugly | Rapsody</u>

They tried to erase our bloodline
Like mistakes written in pencil
They failed to realize
Our history,
Carved in stone
Painted in Hieroglyphics
Vivid depictions
That passed the test of time
With honors
Despite the lies
they fed our minds
From generations down
The truth always
Found its way to light
Now, we use our sorrow
To create new history
For a brighter tomorrow

Michael Tavon

No Church in the Wild | Jay Z, Kanye, Frank Ocean

On an easy Sunday morning
My granny,
Took us to service
It wasn't much,
Just a small wooden house
Converted into a church,
The choir sang off-key,
The pastor shouted
Til his voice cracked
The summer heat intensified
Through the windows
Like an oven light,
As we slowly baked
In our pews
We swallowed a swig
Of Jesus' blood,
And ate a chunk of stale bread
Things quickly got strange,
For my young eyes,
A few of from the flock
Kneeled before the pulpit
As the revered shouted verses
And smeared holy oil
On their foreheads,
Some members fainted
While others seized
And foamed
At the mouth
like diseased raccoons

Songs for Each Mood II

"Y'all stand up,"
Granny demanded,
As she didn't want to clap
And praise alone,
But we were afraid,
We thought those
Foaming monsters
Were going to bite us,
So we stood,
Joined by the hands
With our eyes
Closes until service ended
Later on,
While stuffing soul food
down our throats,
The sound of shattering glass
Fluttering papers & hard impact
Echoed from the pastor's office
Everyone rushed
To see the commotion,
It was the pastor & an usher
Entangled while
Choking & throwing haymakers
Inflicting damage like a hurricane.
Everyone scattered
like ants avoiding the storm
For a long time
I believed church was a terrible place

Hopeful | Twista & Faith Evans

Life flows in waves
Some shallow enough
to see through
Other waves try to swallow you alive

Some waves are soothing
& will gently guide you when lost
Some will crash heavily down
Forcing you to survive alone

There's a blessing to be found
in each wave if you don't drown

Never lose sight
Of your shore
Always swim good like Frank,
Oceans have a way
of keeping you safe
When you feel hopeless

Don't give up,
You may feel like a castaway,
but after the waves subside
you will find your way back home

Songs for Each Mood II

Hey Mama | Kanye West

We often butt heads
Like ram fights
But I'll never lose sight
Of the times you went
The extra mile for me
When you only had
A few inches to spare

When I floated
too deep in the clouds
You were the rock
that anchored me back to earth
When it was time to

You were my life raft
That helped me stay afloat
When I was drowning,
Because I couldn't swim
through life alone

And you were never
Afraid to
write the reality checks
My ass needed to cash

Often times,
I was a sarcastic smart ass
Who forgot to take out the chicken
Or do the dishes
Because I was too busy
Doing nothing

Michael Tavon

I know
Deep down, you wanted
To wring my neck
Like a washcloth
When I got outta line,
Somehow, you never did

Being a mother
Is a job that offers
No vacations or pay raises
But you showed up for me every day
And still do,

As PAC once said:
"There's no way I can pay you back,
But the plan is to show
 you that I understand
You are appreciated."

U, Black Maybe | Common

Am I black enough? I once asked myself

Growing up confused
My fellow skinfolk
said, 'my nigga'
When they greeted me,
But my English
Was crystal clear like Bahama beach water,
my jump shot grazed
more air than a stray bullet
When I yelled "Kobe,"
I couldn't roller skate,
With southern bounce
My feet lacked the rhythm of jazz,
I never rocked,
Retro Jordan's on my toes
I felt out of place in Girbauds
My boxers,
Were never exposed

white boy,
White nigga
Oreo
Carlton
Is what they all called me
White people too.

"Why isn't my black valid enough?"

Michael Tavon

I asked myself
I'd drown in the deep
end of the pool
I'd get killed by the cops too.
I love Lil Wayne,
I watch Martin too,

How am I not black enough?
What does being black mean?
How do I become that?
Questions I could
never find the answer too
Because they didn't exist

It took me a long time
Before I discovered
The nuance of blackness,
We're magic,
Multifaceted,
Can't be reduced to
One idea,
Language,
Or perspective

This I wish I knew before
social anxiety suffocated me
Every time I tried to socialize
With my own people

Mathematics | Mos Def

Bullets kill sons
Bullets kill fathers
Bullets kill mothers
Bullets kill daughters

Bullets kill for revenge
Bullets kill for fun
Bullets rob the rich
Bullets rob the poor

Bullets fuck the nuns
Billers fuck the whores
Bullets visit churches
Bullets visit schools

Bullets break the peace
Bullets break the rules
Bullets are colorblind
Bullets are fools

Bullets don't discriminate
people behind the trigger do

The sad truth,
No matter where you go
Or who you are,
A bullet may find you

I'll Be Missing You | Diddy

Ma' made a tradition
Out of celebrating
her children's existence
with confetti and sunshine
as our time on earth burn slow
like the candles
we blew our dreams
and wishes to
Birthdays,
are reminders
To appreciate each day
Because the biggest blessing
Is blowing out the candles
That symbolizes time

Six Hustles | Larry June

The Story:

A homeless man,
On the highway
Holding a sign that read
"Homeless...need food."
His cup,
full of cash

A young woman's
GoFundMe link
Goes viral after crying
for donations towards
a plane ticket back home
She was stranded in Atlanta
And raised over $10,000

anonymous accounts
gained attention
For accusing Bieber,
And Cole Sprouse
Of sexual misconduct
In 20 minutes
They were guilty
in the court of public opinion.

Michael Tavon

Reality:

That homeless man,
Was cursing, "I don't have a fucking car,"
To his iPhone.

The young woman
Spent her weekend clubbing
Chasing after athletes
In high heels
On all-star weekend

Those anons
Admitted to fabricating
Their stories then deleted
Their accounts

Lessons learned:

Some people
have garbage hearts
And will do anything
To take advantage
Of other's goodwill

This is why,
We can't be
Naive
And quick to believe
Everything we see or read

Stressed Out | A Tribe Called Quest

I was the kid,
Who broke out in hives
The night before
The first day of school
I guess I was allergic
To new beginnings,
As my alarm clock
Told me to go to sleep
I could only imagine
A million things that could go wrong

I was the kid,
Whose mind drew a blank for
Every big test,
Even when
The answers
Slapped my face
a voice would say
"It's a trick; pick something else."

I was the kid

Who rehearsed
A thousand different ways
To ask out my crush

But when we crossed
paths each morning
I struggled to put the words together
Like a bad game of scrabble

I was the kid,
Who hid in a shell
Because I was afraid
To expose my true self
Being vulnerable,
Was like living in a glass home
Surrounded by stones
I spent most of my youth
It was just *bad nerves*
Because *anxiety*
Didn't exist in my community

Heaven ain't Hard to Find | 2Pac

Anxiety has a way of confining you inside
The walls you've built and calling it a sanctuary.
After a while, this place becomes such a cozy home
you have no desire to step outside to smell the
flowers blooming around you. Your fears fester into
a façade that convinces your mind; everything is fine.
The thought of stepping outside your comfort zone
creates earthquakes in your stomach but allowing
your anxiety to control your fate is no way to live.
Today, be bold the sun and her clouds are eager to
meet you.

Lockdown | Anderson. Paak

The night sky is covered with freckles
Just like you
As I trace new constellations
On your face
You smile wondering
What my mind
Is designing
With the stars
on your skin

Sunny Daze | Matteo Rossanese

Once you see the beauty
In starting over,
Letting go will
seem less painful

You may think life
Is upside down
But it's a chance
To view it all from a different angle

It's okay to feel upset
My friend,
But don't let that heart
Burn with anger

this is far from the end
Moving on is a blessing
When grief doesn't kill
It turns demons into angels

Can't Believe It | T-Pain & Lil Wayne

Tossing rocks into the ocean,
Dancing in the sand,
Conversations with the clouds
Only the sky would understand

Take me by the hand,
Never drift away,
You and I under the sun
Getting kissed by the rays

Songs for Each Mood II

Bonus Tracks:

Michael Tavon

Don't Wanna Try | Frankie J

It's not about who's right or wrong
It's about expressing our hearts
Without getting hurt
There's no need to
Yell or curse

Can we mute our egos
And set our prides to the side
To do what's right
I don't want to fight and cry tonight

Let's openly vocalize empathy
To kill this negative energy
Between you and me

We need a heart to heart,
Until we can see eye to eye
Our love is too deep
To drown on the shallow side
Of a fight

Pretty Wings | Maxwell

Despite, how swiftly my heart
Fell for you

There's no bitter after taste
For your sudden demise

I won't cry

or beg for closure .
No more punch-drunk love
I'm better off sober

If you ever decide to reach out, again
You won't feel my touch in return

You are another lesson learned,
Another bridge burned

I will let your wings fly
So please do not return

Gone | N Sync

Your pride blinded you
from seeing your mistakes clearly.

The way you cracked my
Heart open a thousand times,
Should've been a crime.

Ego was the cause of death
Between us,
Because saying sorry
Would've torn you apart

They say love
 is stronger than pride
but to you
love isn't worth
putting out the fire you caused

Printed in Great Britain
by Amazon